FINGERPICKING
HIT SONGS

Arrangements by Tom Huizinga

ISBN 978-1-4950-6425-8

7777 W. BLUEMOUND RD. P.O. BOX 13819 MILWAUKEE, WI 53213

Visit Hal Leonard Online at
www.halleonard.com

Apologize

Words and Music by Ryan Tedder

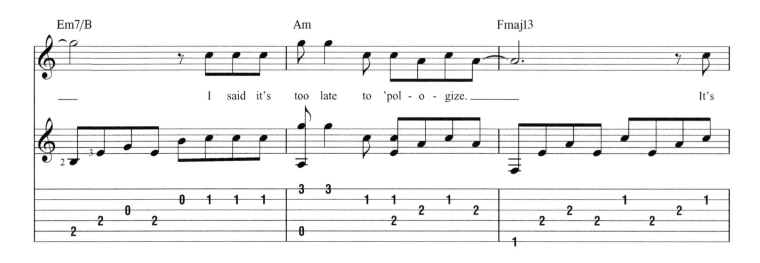

I said it's too late to 'pol - o - gize. _____ It's

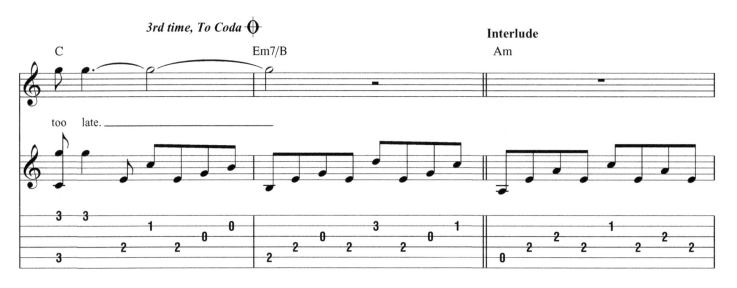

3rd time, To Coda ⊕

Interlude

too late. _____

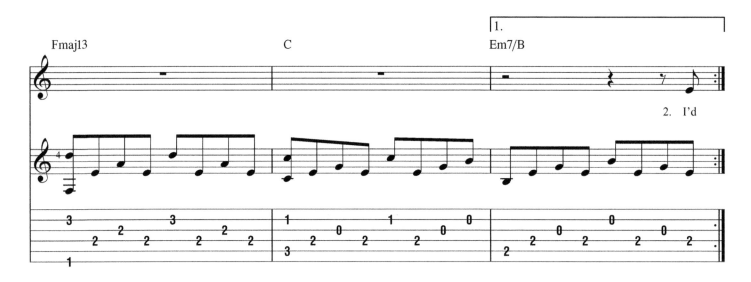

1.

2. I'd

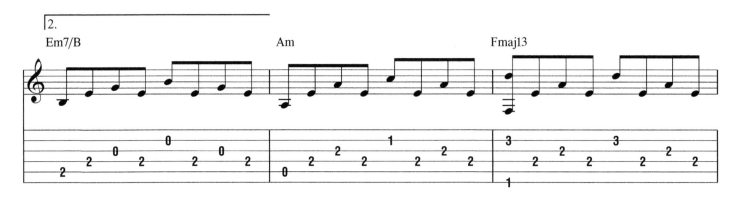

2.

Blank Space

Words and Music by Taylor Swift, Max Martin and Shellback

*Spoken:
I can make the bad guys good for a weekend.
darling, I'm a nightmare dressed like a daydream.

So it's gon-na be for-ev-er or it's gon-na go down in flames. __

*Lyrics in italics are spoken.

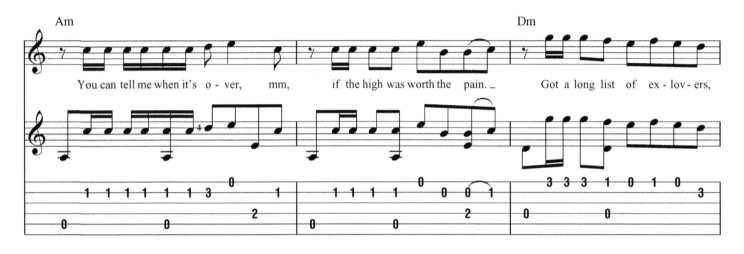

You can tell me when it's o-ver, mm, if the high was worth the pain. __ Got a long list of ex-lov-ers,

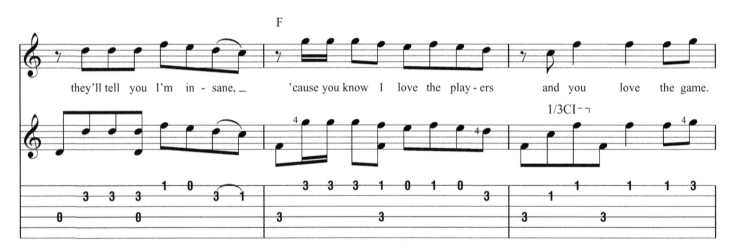

they'll tell you I'm in-sane, __ 'cause you know I love the play-ers and you love the game.

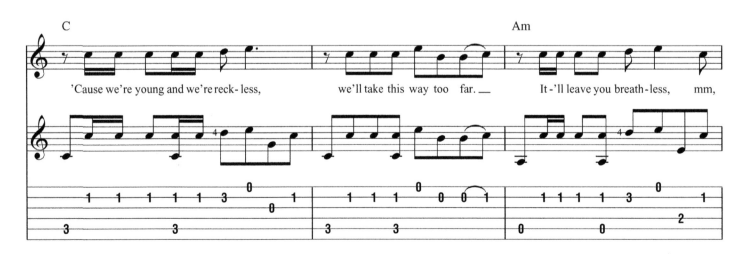

'Cause we're young and we're reck-less, we'll take this way too far. __ It-'ll leave you breath-less, mm,

Chasing Cars

Words and Music by Gary Lightbody, Tom Simpson, Paul Wilson, Jonathan Quinn and Nathan Connolly

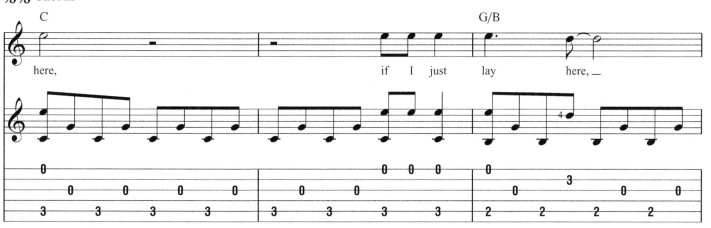

Chorus

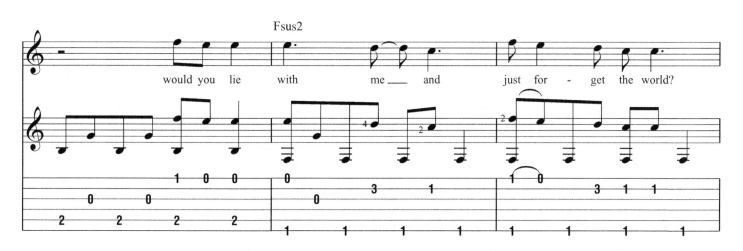

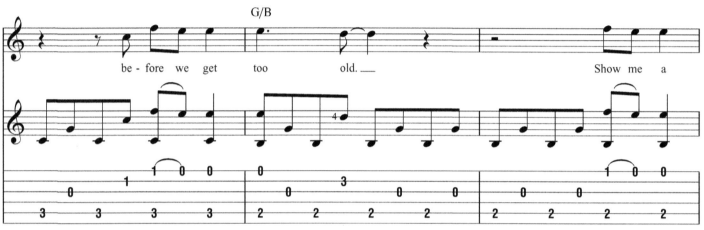

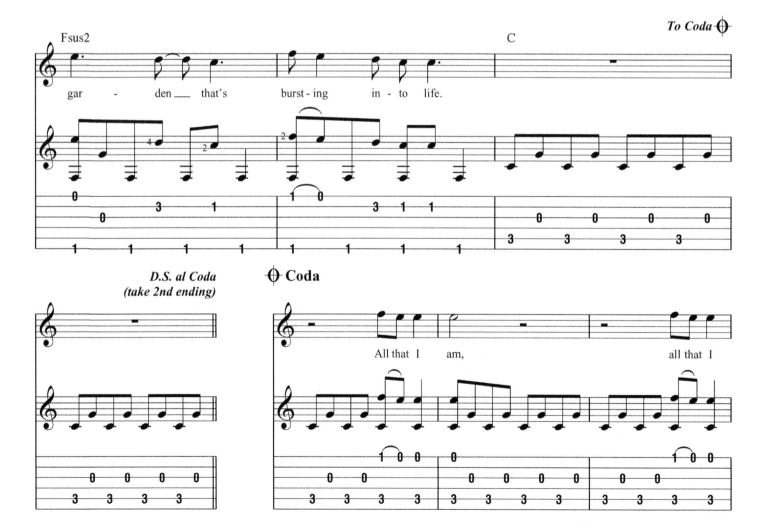

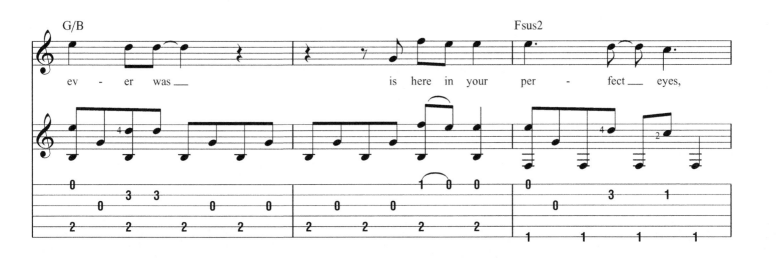

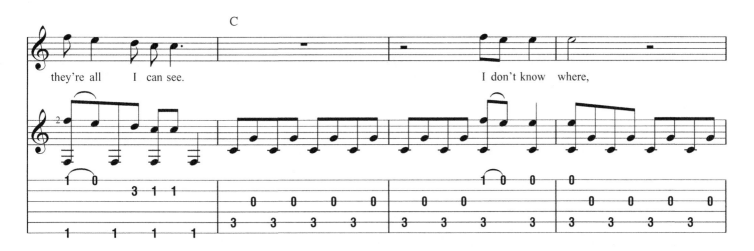

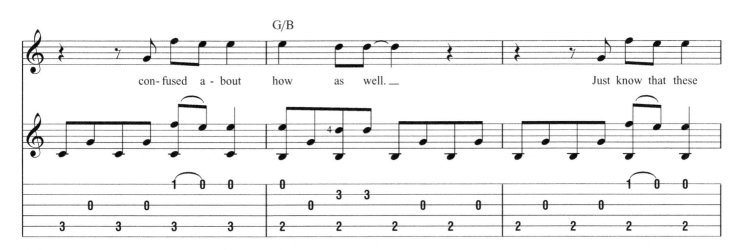

D.S.S. al Fine
(take 1st ending)

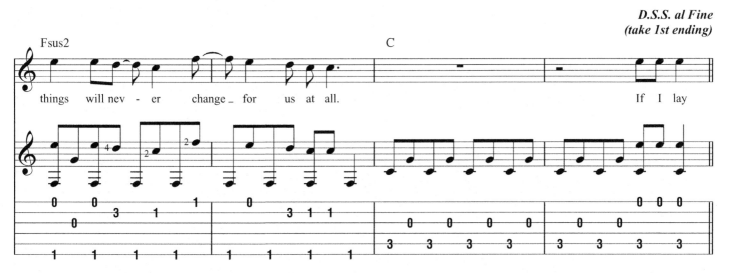

Hello

Words and Music by Adele Adkins and Greg Kurstin

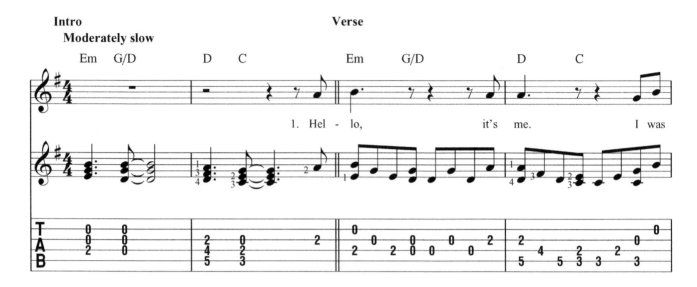

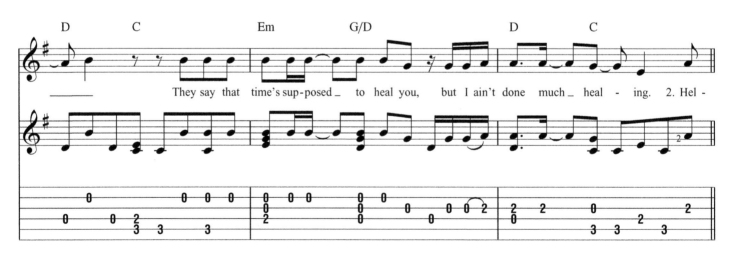

17

% Chorus

I'm Not the Only One

Words and Music by Sam Smith and James Napier

Verse

2. For months on end I've had my doubts,
3. You've been so un-a-vail-a-ble,

de-ny-ing ev-'ry tear. I wish this would be
now sad-ly I know why. Your heart is un-ob-

o-ver now, but I know ___ that I still need you ___ here. ___
tain-a-ble e-ven though ___ Lord knows you kept mine. ___ You

Chorus

say I'm cra-zy 'cause you don't think I know what you've done. ___

I'm Yours

Words and Music by Jason Mraz

more, no more. It can - not wait. I'm yours.

1st time only

Interlude

Verse

2. Well, o - pen up your mind and see ___ like me.   O - pen up your plans and, damn, ___ you're free.
4. Well, o - pen up your mind and see ___ like me.   O - pen up your plans and, damn, ___ you're free.

Let Her Go

Words and Music by Michael David Rosenberg

Only know you've been high when you're feel-ing low. On-ly hate the

road when you're miss-ing home. On-ly know you love her when you let her go.

Interlude

And you let her go. —

Let It Go

Words and Music by James Bay and Paul Barry

Pre-Chorus

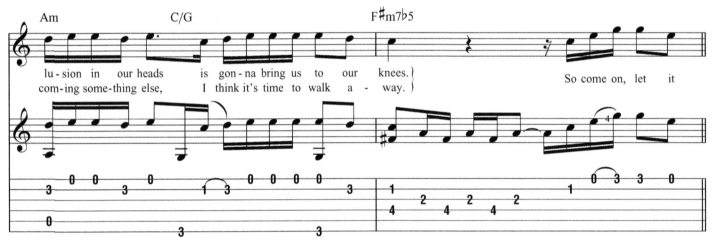

Chorus

Bridge

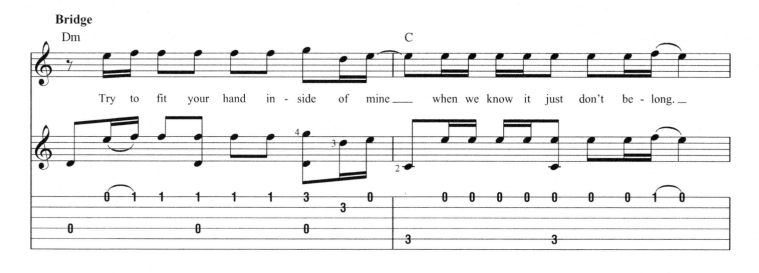

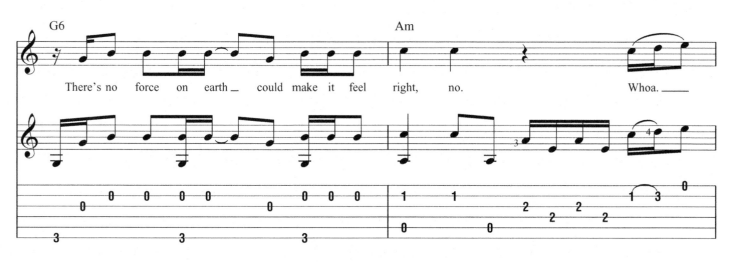

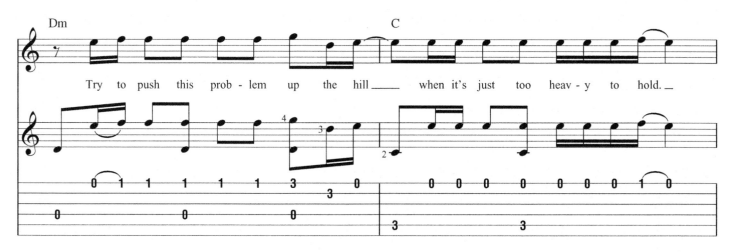

D.S. al Coda

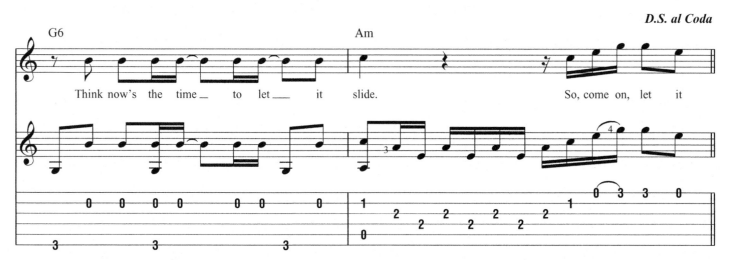

Love Yourself

Words and Music by Justin Bieber, Benjamin Levin and Ed Sheeran

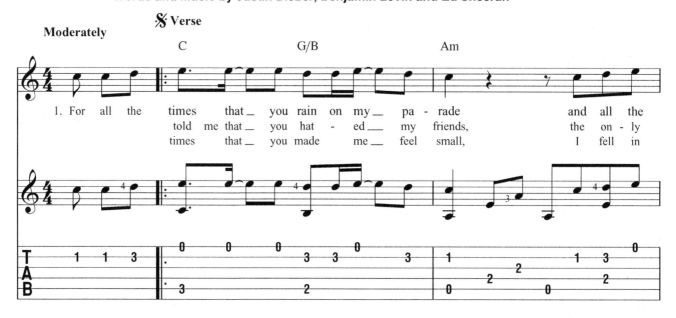

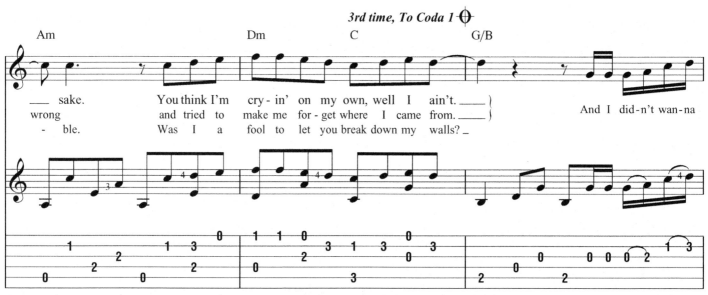

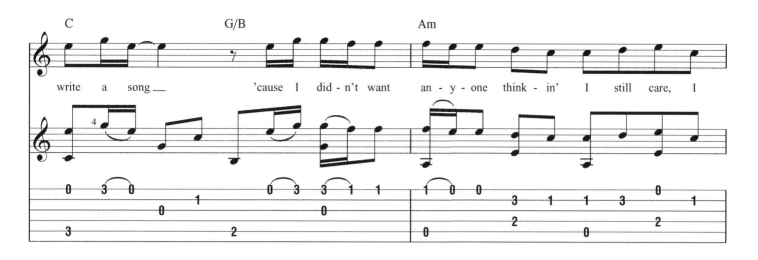

write a song __ 'cause I did-n't want an-y-one think-in' I still care, I

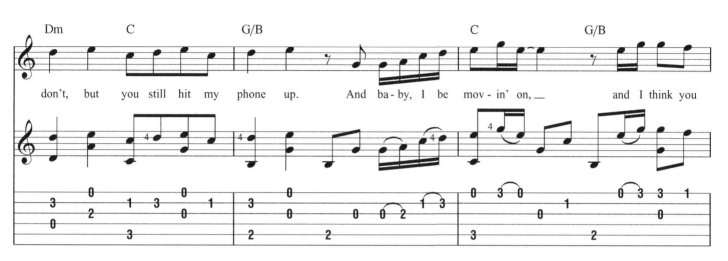

don't, but you still hit my phone up. And ba-by, I be mov-in' on, __ and I think you

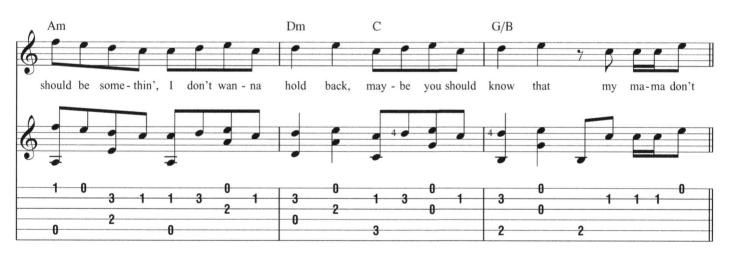

should be some-thin', I don't wan-na hold back, may-be you should know that my ma-ma don't

Pre-Chorus

like you and she likes ev-er-y-one. And I nev-er like to ad-mit that I __ was

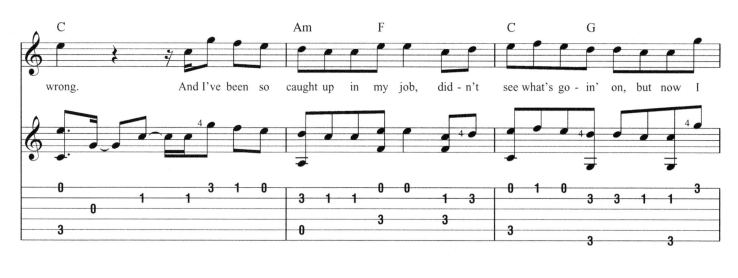

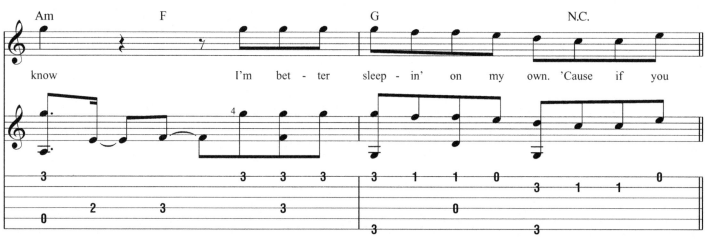

𝄋𝄋 Chorus

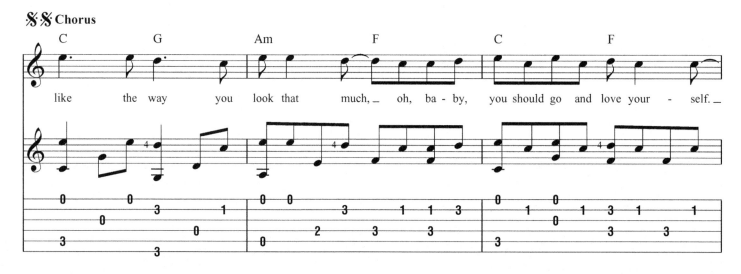

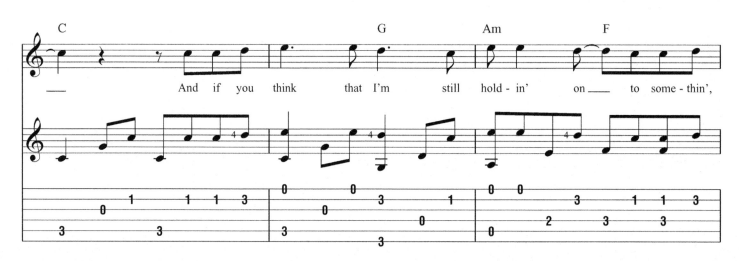

Night Changes

Words and Music by Louis Tomlinson, Liam Payne, Niall Horan,
Zayn Malik, Harry Styles, Julian Bunetta, Jamie Scott and John Ryan

But there's noth-ing to be ____ a - fraid ___ of; e - ven when the night ____ chang - es, ____

1.
it will nev - er change ___ me and you. ____

2.
Interlude
____ me and you. ____

46

Additional Lyrics

2. Chasing it tonight; doubts are runnin' 'round her head.
He's waiting; hides behind a cigarette.
Heart is beatin' loud, and she doesn't want it to stop.
Moving too fast; moon is lighting up her skin.
She's falling, doesn't even know it yet.
Having no regrets is all that she really wants.

Stressed Out

Words and Music by Tyler Joseph

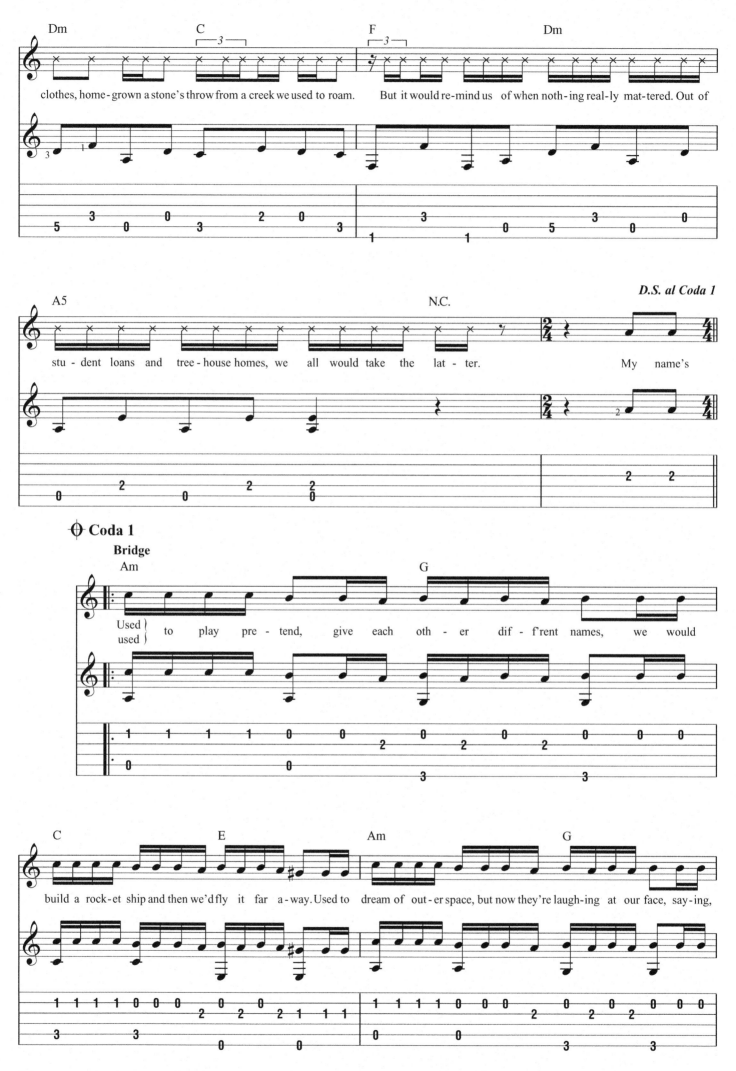

Radioactive

Words and Music by Daniel Reynolds, Benjamin McKee, Daniel Sermon, Alexander Grant and Josh Mosser

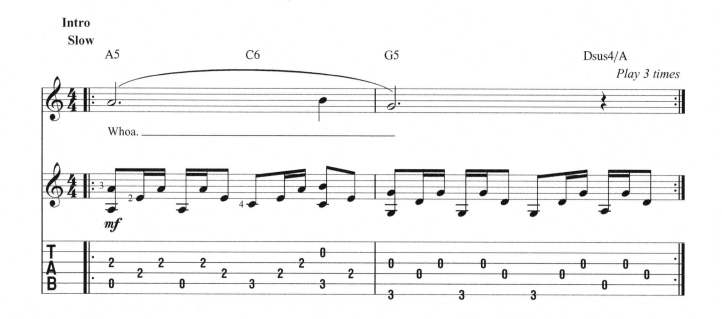

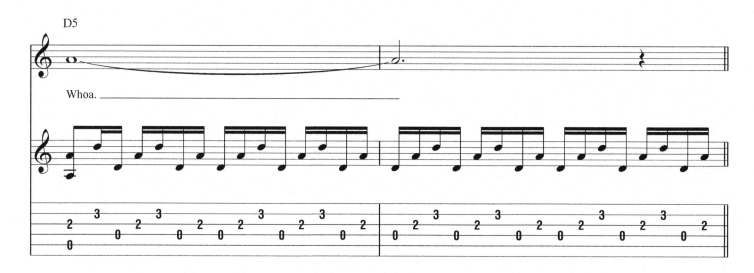

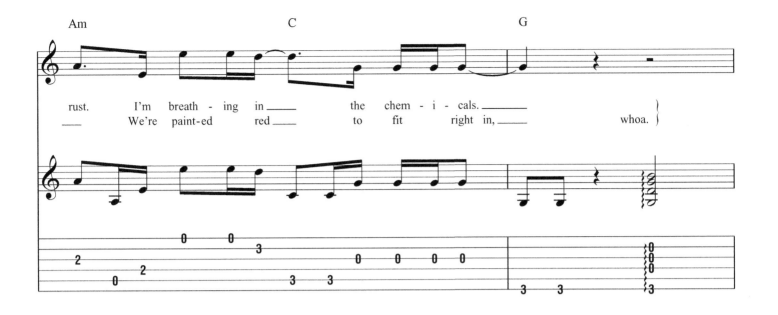

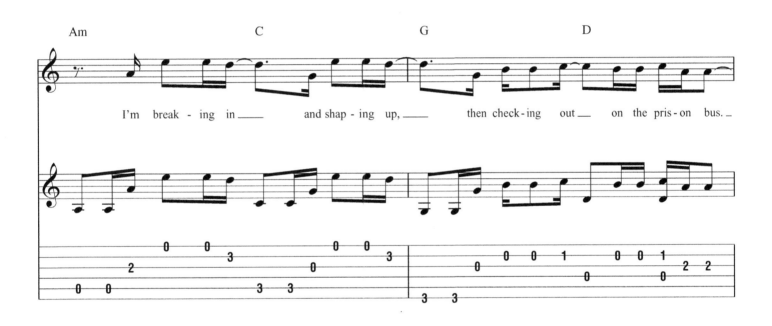

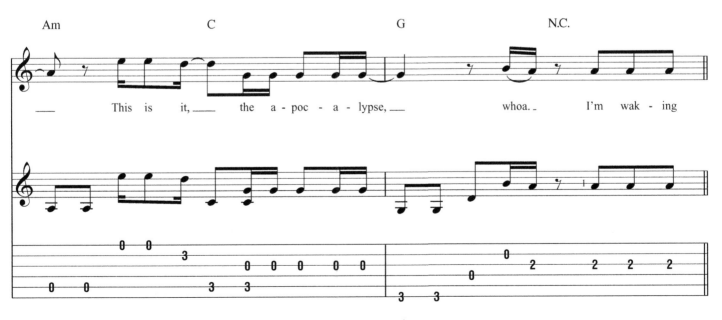

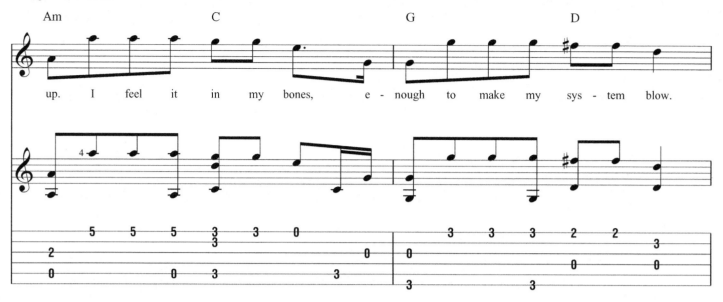

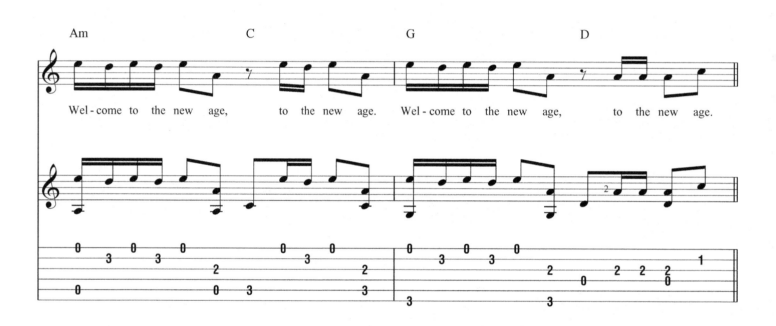

Chorus

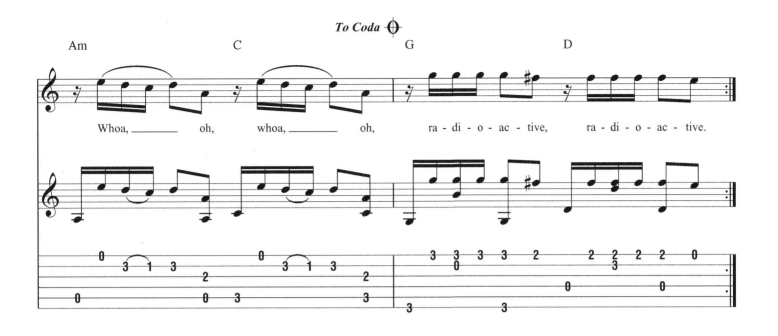

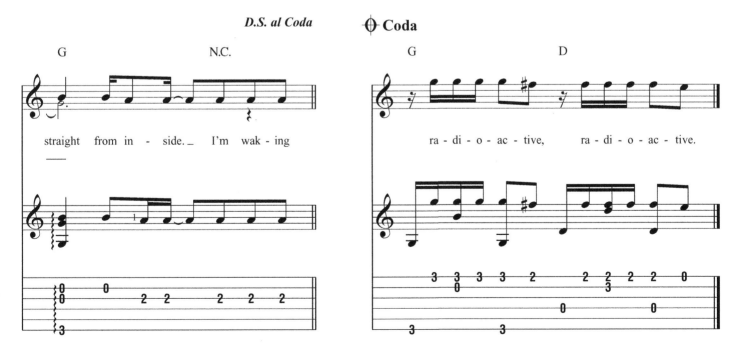

The Scientist

Words and Music by Guy Berryman, Jon Buckland, Will Champion and Chris Martin

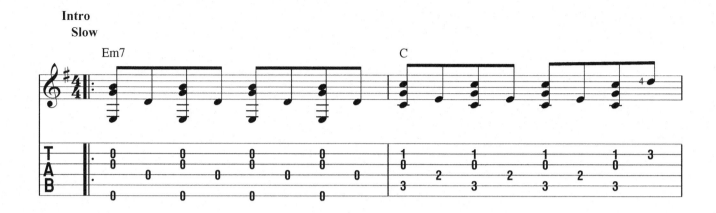

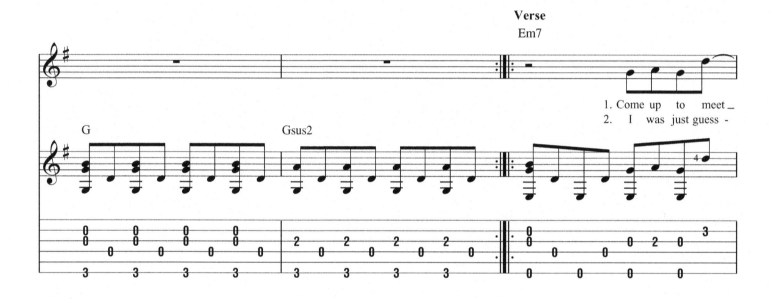

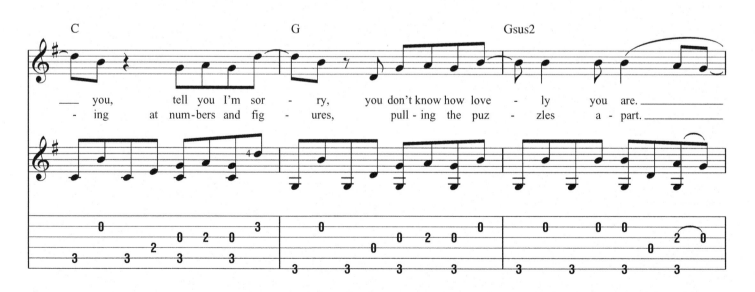

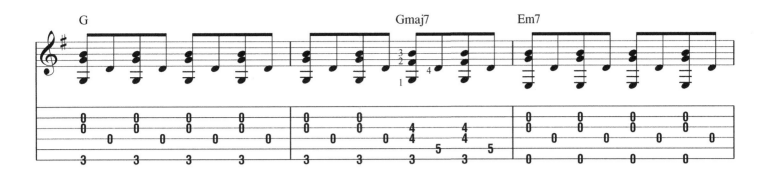

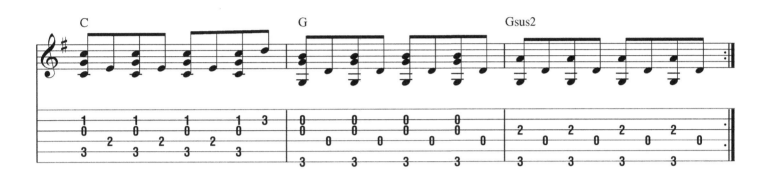

Outro

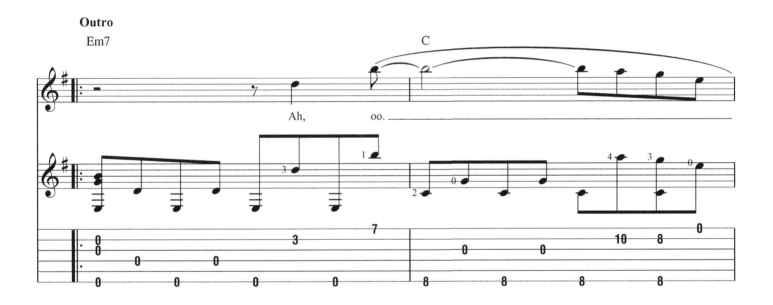

Ah, oo.

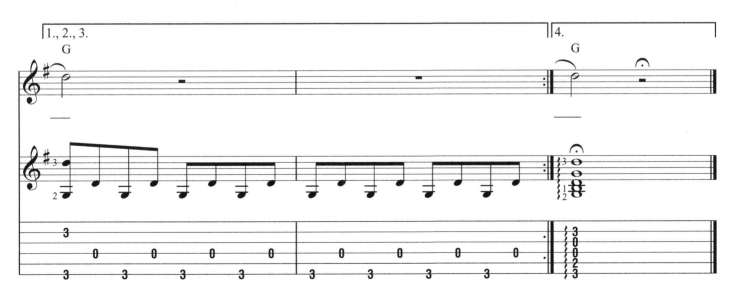

Thinking Out Loud

Words and Music by Ed Sheeran and Amy Wadge

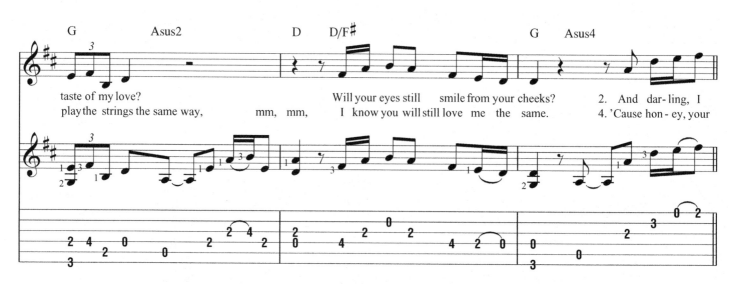

64

A Thousand Years

from the Summit Entertainment film THE TWILIGHT SAGA: BREAKING DAWN - PART 1

Words and Music by David Hodges and Christina Perri

Intro
Moderately fast

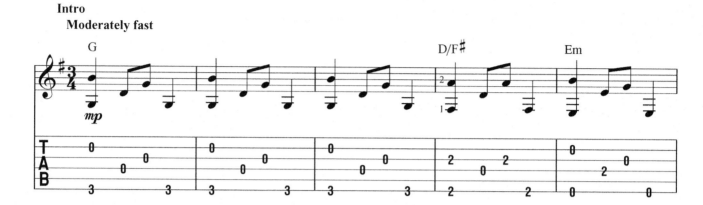

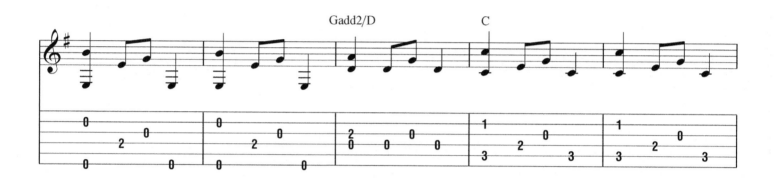

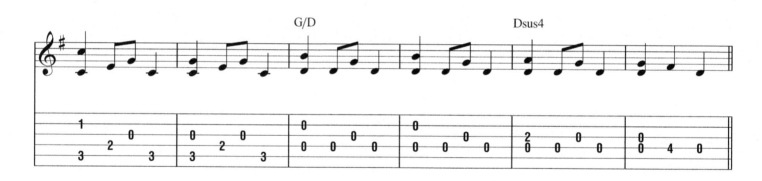

Verse

1. Heart   beats   fast.   Col - ors   and   prom -
2. Time   stands   still,   beau - ty   in   all

INTRODUCTION TO FINGERSTYLE GUITAR

Fingerstyle (a.k.a. fingerpicking) is a guitar technique that means you literally pick the strings with your right-hand fingers and thumb. This contrasts with the conventional technique of strumming and playing single notes with a pick (a.k.a. flatpicking). For fingerpicking, you can use any type of guitar: acoustic steel-string, nylon-string classical, or electric.

THE RIGHT HAND

The most common right-hand position is shown here.

Use a high wrist; arch your palm as if you were holding a ping-pong ball. Keep the thumb outside and away from the fingers, and let the fingers do the work rather than lifting your whole hand.

The thumb generally plucks the bottom strings with downstrokes on the left side of the thumb and thumbnail. The other fingers pluck the higher strings using upstrokes with the fleshy tip of the fingers and fingernails. The thumb and fingers should pluck one string per stroke and not brush over several strings.

Another picking option you may choose to use is called hybrid picking (a.k.a. plectrum-style fingerpicking). Here, the pick is usually held between the thumb and first finger, and the three remaining fingers are assigned to pluck the higher strings.

THE LEFT HAND

The left-hand fingers are numbered 1 through 4.

Be sure to keep your fingers arched, with each joint bent; if they flatten out across the strings, they will deaden the sound when you fingerpick. As a general rule, let the strings ring as long as possible when playing fingerstyle.

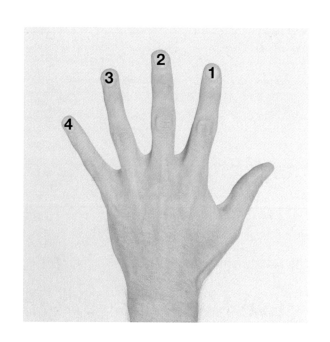